Escaping the Cage

Kate Scott

Happen*Stance*

Poems © Kate Scott, 2010
Cover image © Gillian Beaton, 2010
ISBN 978-1-905939-53-4
All rights reserved.

Acknowledgements:
Thanks are due to editors of the following publications, in which some of these poems first appeared: *Agenda, Magma, New Walk Magazine, The New Writer, Poetry Nottingham, The Rialto.* Some of the poems were written during a residency for the National Trust (with Paul Hyland, Catherine Simmonds and Pam Zinnemann-Hope) as part of the Poetry Society Centenary celebrations in 2009.

Also by Kate Scott:
- *Stitches*, Peterloo Poets, 2003
- *Who's in the Next Room?* (with Paul Hyland, Catherine Simmonds and Pam Zinnemann-Hope), Happen*Stance*, 2010

Published in 2010 by Happen*Stance*
21 Hatton Green, Glenrothes, Fife KY7 4SD
nell@happenstancepress.com
www.happenstancepress.com

Printed by The Dolphin Press
www.dolphinpress.co.uk

Orders:
Individual pamphlets £4.00 (includes UK P&P).
Please make cheques payable to Happen*Stance* or order through PayPal in the website shop.

Contents ∾

First Proposal	5
Outing	6
Escaping the Cage	8
His sightless gaze	9
When you pressed your palms	10
Jealousy	11
All the men I've never slept with	12
Caged	13
Barometer	14
Relief	15
Some Afternoons	16
Blind	17
Introduction	18
Smile	19
Not Eating	20
Another Folk Song	21
Coasting	22
History	23
Survival	24
Crime Scene	26
Whitewash	27
Sometimes	28
Ghosts	29
The Making of the Lady of the Lake	30
Start	32

for my father

First Proposal

He tasted like oysters
and I had never liked oysters
but then he moved,
strained like an impatient colt against the rein,
broke me, and in the flame of pain
I felt a high of relief,
recognised the gasping distance.

It was the first serious thing I had done:
my skin handgliding alive,
my body stripped and panting
to an exhilarated core,
every cell shaking with its just-hatched power.

So when he clutched me against him,
asked me to marry him—almost tearful—
nuzzling astounded, so grateful in my hair,
I turned myself
and my swoop-hearted secret
tight against his neck,

wanting to do nothing

but laugh.

Outing

It's the perfect day for it.
His mother is all smiles and sandwiches
while his dad looms over the blanket
because they don't know enough
to stop trying.

The boy's old enough to be resigned
but his sister's pumped up high
on hormones and disgust.
It's a moment of spite, pure
and simple:
So why didn't you ask your boyfriend to come?

He sees the question slide from her mouth,
a sly knife into his father's jowls,
his mother's plump, unsuspecting side.
He turns to see his mother's everyday face
stung with Greek tragedy: *no grandchildren*
while his father's eyes flutter, then rattle shut,
his legs stiffening as he turns.

The boy rises up slowly, stumbles like a new-born calf,
his sister slack-mouthed as the cows nearby.
He's never liked her.
He leans against the nearest gate,
feels the top bar give
as he stares into the sea-sick grass,
the trees tipping in the wind.

He imagines running,
the cut cord of his family flapping behind.
He thinks of all the bends in the road
they followed to get here,
almost smiles.

Escaping the Cage

I liked to hold them in my mouth
like some hard-boiled sweet
I was about to crack.
I sat with my close-held lips,
my wide shiny eyes;
the delicate spray of roses across my skirt,
the filigree of fingers on my placid lap,
the long hair looped behind my ears,
all spelling acceptable words.
I liked to smile,
one surface gleaming at another.

And then I liked to let them rip:
a surge of expletives like a glorious fart,
a magnificent belch,
hard and fast in quick succession,
splintering the air between us.
I loved the electric forks of shock,
loved to hear the box around me split,
to see tight smiles slip,
eyes not knowing where to fix.
I liked to feel I had done my duty
as I raised one, long, clean finger
to adjust the rounded collar
of my light white blouse.

His sightless gaze,

his little boy stance,
scorched her lungs,
her heart flaring to protective flame.
Her body itched to surround him,
to bake his blood warm.
But drink by drink he froze over,
dropped deep from the sense of himself
or who she could be to him

and the reality soaked in—
only he could focus beyond the glass,
only he could put the stopper in what flowed in
and what flowed out.
Even as she blazed her own poison,
his empty glance silenced her lips
as sure as his fingers.
She felt herself slammed like a shot
with his face ice-blind against her
and anything her heart could say.

When you pressed your palms

gently, to each side of my face,
and looked down at me, sadly
but smiling,
I wanted to hit you.
Against my will, I kept crying,
the wad of pride
at the back of my clenching jaw.

But after you left, with me retching
at all you'd said and done
and how I'd done
nothing but cry,
yes, after you left, I swallowed that wad of pride
and felt it unfurl,
felt it stretch out the way an orchid sketches itself
or the wings of a moth unfold at birth
to several times its body's size.

It was magnificent, it filled my blood, it was glorious, like fire.
It was something to be reckoned with—my sense of self—
coming back to home.

Jealousy

He sends me love poems,
love poems for a woman
who is not his wife.
He sends me poems about his wife:
not a woman he loves.
And I am another woman torn
between the girl who feels the ghost
of his lips at her throat
and the wife who watches with slanted eyes
his silent count of longing.

And there are children,
of course there are children
waiting backstage in this,
their hurt waiting its cue
for a main part in this play of lies.
And she is . . . but I cannot quote him,
I should not quote him.
Every line is sculptured agony,
a stunning spine-curl of pain.

So if I was given a whistle,
would I blow or hold my breath?
Because it's not held
for him, or his wife,
the other, the children;
but for the sake of those words,
the beautiful, beautiful words.

All the men I've never slept with

gather in the room.
I run my fingers down their runner-bean spines
to their apple-tight buttocks, their courgette thighs.
Their skins are glistening—dark as aubergine,
pale as parsnip.
How they would dance:
two-four, four-four, eight!
I count and count and count.

And then you get up:
the men scatter to the walls, rattled like dry rice.
Strolling past, you lay your hand upon my head,
brand me with your warmth,
and all the men I've never slept with
go passing through the chink in the door,
slip into the untasted night.

Caged

He's sucked tight to my nipple, grazing the flesh
with a lone tooth, uttering his grunt-sung sighs.
One fat hand grabs my ribs,
the other slaps my breast;
a hungry paw against a deer's trapped flank.

She's yowling at a graze, pulling down tights
to show her wound, lashing out splayed hair and fingers.
She winds her complaints around my legs,
a snake winding me tighter
and tighter and tighter.

Such animals, my girl, my boy;
such a scattering of legs and arms
from room to room.
I track their screeches, whines and cries.
Then all at once—
momentary hush—
their soft underbellies,
their sweaty skin,
their sticky, needy hands.

I'm caught in a second by the sudden softenings,
the ambush of smiles after hours of monsoons.
As I put him behind the rails of his cot,
tuck her behind the guard of her bed,
I don't know who in this house
is behind bars.

Barometer

He raps the gauge smartly,
sure and hard, like his feet in 1942
when he did the jive with his girl in rose.
Later, she flicked an imaginary thread from her skirt
before raising her head to meet his kiss,
their lips urgent with the war within,
their outlines hard against each other,
the band's *We'll meet again*
floating out and up through the open door.

And later, the switch of his temper,
when in the height he said *I fought the war for you* and his son said
And do you think it was worth it? and laughed and laughed
until the laugh slammed shut
behind his hard back hand.

And later again how he'd stood
in the narrow vein of the hall,
flicking the light switch on, off, on, off,
on the night she died—an aneurysm,
some blockage of light.

And so, when his granddaughter asks him
What makes the silver rise? and he answers *Pressure*,
he means *love*.

Relief

Driving home after *such a nice time, must
do it again soon.* A tone she mistrusts.
He swears as the rain starts.
The children sing *buggerbugger* in the back.
There's an hour ahead of *which way, but you said left.*

She leans her head against the cold glass
as if to press the strain in, blot the
stop that, be quiet, I'm warning you out.
He is sighing in the way that makes her knuckles tight.
The children are singing *buggerbugger* in the back.

They pull up at a smear of red, and she looks down to see
a small pool of rain holding a shiver of light.
He begins to whistle a tune she loves
as the children sweetly sing
buggerbugger in the back.

Some Afternoons

Some afternoons I take her out in the car.
We go fast. Fast, with the windows down,
the wind winding its fingers round
our hair, its palms pressed hard
against our cheeks.
I drive to feel the brief unfastening
from this life of close-knit tasks.
She laughs at the wind, at the slant of sun
playing on her face. This is a run,
dreaming of driving to the edge, and then beyond.
I can see the rooms where we would stay:
camel-humped beds and crumbling wallpaper;
the glass of wine in the bar; me suddenly sexy
in another language, wearing her like an accessory,
light as a bracelet. For this is about weight,
the weight of a life, the daub and mottle of walls
that last, and when running you shed things,
like a snake with his snake hide behind him.
I begin to brake without thinking;
the pull is acceleration in reverse.
We are meshed in the home walls,
this small child and I,
the hair and earth of its frame.
We are balancing on a world
that keeps turning,
however fast we run.

Blind

Catching the eye, watching the lip,
running the glance up the leg to the crotch
used to be the game.
How far you could go before meeting
pupil to pupil,
dilated, smiling.
Possibility was everywhere,
no route so small you couldn't find it.
Even getting the milk could mean a cheap
erotic kick.
I learned the language of wide eyes and teasing fingers,
brushing the hem of a sleeve,
a body sentence of *yes*.

But now I board trains, planes, buses,
sit in traffic humming at the lights,
stroll down the street like some miracle
of perambulation,
eyes pinned straight ahead.
Seeing you folded next to my heart
I am blind, blind, blind.

Introduction

Each day I try a different self,
none feeling quite right;
a snake stuck in the wrong skin,
a teenager stuck in an inappropriate pose.
When not in use, the other selves
stand round together, whispering
and commenting on my current choice.

Today I am a mother.
I hold her in my hands:
this familiar stranger,
this genetic reflection.

The thought comes that she isn't mine,
I am hers, all hers.
The selves are placing bets
but when I turn round
they begin to fuse.
She grasps my finger
and I begin myself at last.

Something else is being born here.
My daughter is giving back a life,
a tooth for a tooth,
an I for an I.

Smile

You smile and my stomach swells.
My voice swept high with almost-tears, I ask
Is that a smile?
(arrival of child, disappearance of brain)
Is that a smile?

Your smile loops my heart,
brings me as close to you as we were
before you pushed yourself out of me,
your wise eyes stunned,
your starfish hands opening to our fingers.

An avid reader, I disdain books
for the sight of your intent eyes following space
as you feed on my breast.
I ignore grown-up conversation
to sing back the birth of your vowels and consonants,
your coo and call.

You are my partying heart,
my best reflection,
my widest smile.

Not Eating

The pea protrudes, slowly, on her tongue.
She looks at me deliberately, cool as a cowboy
with her hand on her gun.
The pea falls and I fire. I spit words,
I sputter *Starving children* while she stares me out.
She is sixteen months old. Her vocabulary is three words wide:
mama, dada and *duck*. She cannot stretch
to starving children, or guilt, or my fury.
She can just stretch her tongue
to proffer my food back to me.

She watches impassively while I become
a Vaudevillian, dancing with a spoon,
whistling and choo-choo-ing like a train.
The train is going nowhere:
she has decided on a desert destination,
she is taking no provisions but her own.

What is this need to see her mouth open and close?
To see her lengthen her limbs as she
lengthens the distance between us?
This town is too big, she seems to say,
and even though each inch
is another inch away from us,
I fill the spoon,
I play the fool,
I ache to see the dust
settle on her growth.

Another Folk Song

We are playing a song—people leaving the places they love.
She is dancing and falling, dancing and falling.
We laugh as she stretches up to the door,
already leaving, already trying to close us behind her

but like the chord that strikes the duct—the minor fall,
the major rise—she cries when she fails, reaches out to be held,
and though the song that falls and rises, falls to rise
and lingers on the lines around my husband's eyes,

her thinning cries, rocked to smiles,
seem to be another folk song;
we three—a riff on things that pass—are leaving, dancing:
we rise and fall and fall to rise.

Coasting

Lessons washed right over him,
he kept waiting for something to hold onto
but nothing snagged;
the teachers were the noise of waves beyond a window.

After school he washed up in a supermarket packing house;
tide after tide of life's essentials boxed up,
distributed from him to the world—as if none of it
was essential to him, as if he were tied to the seabed,
too cold to move.

Sometimes he'd have a moment:
after last orders when he leaned blurry on the bar,
the beer frousy in his throat,
the damp mats soaking through to his elbow,
the chatter round him like a foreign tongue.
He'd think, *I should do something*—but then the pint would come
and the words distil to a song he liked well enough
to carry him through to the next day.

Or when waking at four he'd feel anchored by heaviness,
by the same old same old soaking him through.
And even the sting of salt when his mum died,
when his girl left,
when the blankness of mid-afternoon stopped his hands in mid air,
the box suspended, like Atlas holding his weighted sky . . .

when even all this

wasn't enough to make him put his arms out

and swim.

History

It's like teenagers playing Chicken,
scrap skeletons from earlier runs
strewn behind every seat.
Everyone would see them
if they would just turn round.

The windows are wound up tight,
they're revving wild,
they're deaf to the onlookers' roars
and that one lone voice
trapped between the urgent, pressing crowd,
the high, unhappy, unheard cry:
Look out, look out, look out!

Survival
for J W

It will take you shielding yourself
against the darkness
that blinds your heart
and punctures your lungs
so your breath draws quick and bleak and cold.

It will take you listening out hard,
as one listens for deer in the deep-leaved woods,
to the words of courage and love that come your way
falling through the thick branches like spells of light.

It will take you straining to hear these words
against the cacophany of the inane,
the well-meaning-but-clumsy pats of comfort,
the callous, tactless happiness
that bumps into you without looking
as you try to find your way alone.

It will take you seeing your friends,
forgiving them not always understanding,
not always offering
the right words, the right actions,
which you hardly know yourself,
so deep are you among these lonely trees
where you try every path
and see him nowhere.

It will take
the seasoning of trees,
the circles wider round the loss,
the light further from the dark.
It will take growing from the ground,
following the turning days,
taking flight
past the tips of the trees,
finding
new leaves,
life.

Crime Scene

No police to mark it off,
just the skeletons—the swirls in stone—
each rigid spine a notch of time.

Held to ransom, the land gives ground,
a recompense of mile by mile.
But tide by tide, the sea advances,
slicing with each surge and rise.

And any bystander
can see the layers,
the hostages
of petrified bone;
any present witness
can swear to
all that proof
of what's been done.

Whitewash

Inching along the A35,
snow squawking under the tyres,
abandoned lorries skewed across their islands of ice,
the pylons pencil scratches against the sky,
you're seduced a century back.
You can't see the lego housing,
the tractors nosing the B roads,
the beetling of cars . . .
just the tucked-up idyll of the Christmas card,
smoke swirling its signature from inglenook fires,
a pot chortling to itself,
a stretch of starched linen issuing steam.
Never mind the stench of the horses,
their hooves high-booted with mud.
Never mind the chipping of grey ice
in a green-veined bowl.
Never mind the thin blue wail of babies,
and the sculpted faces of children,
their parents like commas crouched over the work.
Let the snow cover it all,
let the fifth-gear life idle in neutral,
let the monstrous beast be put to sleep
for three hours of one morning.
Never mind what's under and what lies behind;
the relief to the eye,
and what it wants to believe,
makes you fall for it anyway.

Sometimes

it weighs you down:
the cancerous cells
doing addition in the blood,
in the veins of someone you love.

Sometimes it weighs you down:
the way people leave,
forgetting to say what they meant to you
before they go.

Sometimes it weighs you down:
your heart,
the things it carries.

Ghosts

The things that shot out of my mouth that night—
serpents, snakes, twin-tongued monsters.
Every expletive known to me
handled like a rapier sword
and piercing the South Circular's roar.

I was twenty-three and on fire.
I had sprouted heads and he couldn't look me in the eyes.
My inhibitions fell like scales—
I was vile, incoherent, terrible, wild.
I was naked and true.

When it was over we shook,
our taut skin flushed and damp,
sure this was the start of forever,
that nebulous measure of time
we knew nothing about.

I look back through the bars of my self,
and long for that cleaving sweat,
that boy in a blue shirt,
that anger scarred into our hearts,
that passion shaming my own pale life,

those people capable of so much love.

The Making of the Lady of the Lake

The black-eyed man found me.
He was a glint of kindness,
handed me a soft belly of bread
and a wrap of warm blanket.

I'd always been a good swimmer,
a quick brown trout escaping
the mud and flies and faces I lived with,
their scooped-out cheeks and clammed mouths.
This will be nothing to you, he said.

The robes he gave me were wisps of mist,
a gust of gauze that made me clasp my hands across my chest
even when he smiled because I had nothing to hide
for I was *All valley and no hills.*

The sword took my breath like a swoop of hawk.
It was solid sun, a firebrand in its hilt.
He magicked it from under his cloak
and made me afraid I'd made a pact with the devil.

He laughed, a roar with a knife in it.
I'm a legend-maker, he said. *And you'll be a line in it.*
There'd be food and wine till I was fat as a full moon.
He pressed a kiss to my lips like a hard coin of promise.

Even through the cloud-window of the lake's surface,
I saw the boy's eyes fire with the words in his ear.
I rose and broke the water to fragments,
shaking with the weight of the sword in my hand.

As the boy grasped it, for a moment I saw his belief doused:
I was just a village girl in goddess clothing.
But desire for the magician flared in us both,
our faith hot enough to dry out doubt.

You're a rare one, Vivian, my magician said.
*He's gone away blind. He'll fight a kingdom of giants
before he's done.* I shivered water on the floor of his hut
as he talked out my heart with his tongue.

The morning after, the imprint of his horse's hooves
by the lip of the lake was all that was left
but back in the village, a cluster of men
were talking me immortal:

a lady who could raise the weapons of kings,
a woman who could breathe water,
a young girl bewitched by the trickery of words.

Start

Naked, legs spread wide upon our bed,
our three-year-old pulls herself apart like fruit,
bends her head
to truly see herself.

You say, *I can't look*
and a slide slams down,
a grimy shadow on the sweet flesh
flushed by her bath.
In a stopped breath I see the computer screen,
a hunched back, a pulling hand,
the half-blocked shots
of newness ready for bruising.

I want to put my hand over the words you just let out,
want to swaddle her in endless white,
want to spit the curdled taste as far as it will go.

In the hung silence
the thwack of a ball
attacks our gate,
teenagers splitting air
with thrumming-steel voices.

Our little girl looks up at us,
quiet and whole,
while we stare at each other
through the layers and layers of leaden clothes.